Climbing the Wall

Tana Reiff

A Pacemaker LifeTimes™ 2 Book

LifeTimes™ 2 Titles

Take Away Three
Climbing the Wall
The Door Is Open
Just for Today
Chicken by Che
Play Money
The Missing Piece

Cover Illustration: Michaela Cooney

ISBN 0-8224-4603-0
Printed in the United States of America

7 8 9 10 11   08 07 06 05 04

1-800-321-3106
www.pearsonlearning.com

Contents

CHAPTER 1

Little Kenny
ran about the room
faster and faster.
He tripped on a rug
and fell against
the window.
He was lucky
not to hurt himself.

"Look at Kenny,"
said his mother, Sue.
"Do you really think
he is ready
for first grade?"

"Of course,"
said Jeff, his father.
"He's six years old.

He's old enough
for first grade."

"Sure,"
said Sue.
"He's old enough.
But look at him.
He's wild.
I don't think
he's ready."

"Boys will be boys,"
said Jeff.

Just then
Kenny broke in.
"I don't have
anything to do,"
he said.

"Dinner will be
ready soon,"
Sue said kindly.

"Why don't you
look at your books
or go watch TV?"

Two minutes later
Kenny was back
in a flash.
"I don't like
what's on TV,"
he said.

"Then go out
and play,"
Jeff laughed.
"A lively boy
like you
needs to stay busy."

Kenny ran
out of the house.

"Kenny never slows down,"
said Sue.

"I just don't know
if he's ready
for school."

"I'm sure
he'll be fine,"
Jeff said.
"Going to school
may even help him
slow down."

A minute later
Kenny called his dad
from the backyard.
"Will you
push me
on the swings?"
he asked.

"I'll be right there,"
Jeff called.

Thinking It Over

1. Do you think
   a child like Kenny
   is ready to go to school?

2. When is a child
   ready to go to school?

3. Do you believe in the saying,
   "Boys will be boys"?

CHAPTER 2

Jeff won out.
Kenny started
first grade.
But right away
he fell behind.
He could not
sit still.
He did not listen
to his teacher,
Miss Tiller.
She would tell him
to sit down.
Kenny would sit down.
But then he would
jump back up again.

Kenny couldn't
keep his mind
on what the class
was doing.

He didn't
finish his work.

He made
a lot of noise.
He bothered
other kids.
He even got
into fights
with them.

Miss Tiller shouted
at Kenny
all the time.
But she was afraid
that something
was wrong.
None of the other children
were as wild
as Kenny.

At last she called
Jeff and Sue.
"Does Kenny

act the same way
at home?"
she asked them.

Jeff and Sue
said yes.
Kenny was always
on the move.

"I want Kenny
to meet Mrs. Pence,"
said Miss Tiller.
"She's a special teacher
who works
with children
who have problems,"
she explained.

"Are you saying
he's crazy?"
Jeff asked.
"Kenny doesn't
have a problem.
He's just
a lively boy."

"Of course
he's not crazy,"
said Miss Tiller.
"But Kenny
causes trouble
for himself
and the other kids,"
she said.
"He needs help."

Finally Jeff and Sue
said OK.
Maybe Mrs. Pence
could help Kenny.
After all,
if he didn't
slow down,
he would never learn.

Thinking It Over

1. In what way
   is Miss Tiller
   a good teacher?

2. Why do schools
   have people like Mrs. Pence?

3. What are three reasons
   some children
   have a hard time learning?

CHAPTER 3

Miss Tiller
talked to Mrs. Pence
about Kenny.
"This child
is climbing the wall,"
she said.
"He's driving me crazy.
He drives
his parents crazy.
He drives
everyone crazy."

Then Miss Tiller
took Kenny
to Mrs. Pence's office.
Mrs. Pence
gave Kenny
two tests.
One checked
how much

Kenny already knew.
The other test checked
how much
Kenny would be able
to learn.

Mrs. Pence
also checked to see
how Kenny saw pictures.
She checked
how Kenny heard things.
She checked
how Kenny played
with blocks.
She wanted to see
how Kenny
took in the world
around him.

The tests
showed Mrs. Pence
some interesting things.
Kenny's eyes and ears

worked just fine.
He was
smart.
But he wasn't learning
because he
could not pay attention
to one thing
at a time.
His mind was
all over the place.

So Mrs. Pence
called Kenny's parents.

"Kenny is
probably hyperactive,"
Mrs. Pence explained.
"A hyperactive child
cannot sit still.
A hyperactive child
cannot keep his mind
on one thing
for long.

For these reasons
it is hard
for a hyperactive child
to learn."

"Are you sure
Kenny is hyperactive?"
Jeff asked.

"He shows
all the signs,"
said Mrs. Pence.
"But there is no way
to know for sure.
However, the tests show
that Kenny is
much like
other hyperactive children."

"Are you saying
we should
put him on drugs?"
asked Jeff.

"I don't want
my son
to be a drug addict."

"A lot of parents
feel that way,"
said Mrs. Pence.
"We will try some
other things first.
Even so,
the medicine that helps
hyperactive children
is different than you think.
It's not like the drugs
that get people hooked
or into trouble.
Don't worry
about that now.
But we need
you two
to help.
Kenny can't get better
all by himself."

Something had to be done
to help Kenny.
Mrs. Pence,
Miss Tiller,
Jeff, and Sue
would all help him.

They knew
it would not
be easy to solve
Kenny's problem.
But they had to try.

Thinking It Over

1. Is there ever a good reason
   to put a child on drugs?

2. What could make a child
   into a drug addict?

3. Why can't Kenny
   just make up his mind
   to get better?

CHAPTER 4

Mrs. Pence
had a plan
for Kenny.
It was
a reward plan.
She started it
right away.

Every day
Kenny brought
a note home
to his parents.
He had to
control himself
in two ways
every day.
If Kenny could sit
in his seat
he wrote "Yes"
on the note.

If he didn't
have a fight
he wrote "Yes"
on the note.
His parents
signed each note.
Then Kenny took each note
back to school.

After writing "Yes"
ten times
he would get a reward.
He could watch
his favorite
TV show.
Or he could have
his favorite dinner.

Jeff and Sue
had to watch
what Kenny ate.
He could not
eat sweets.
He couldn't eat

junk food.
Sweets and junk food
only made
Kenny worse.

The reward plan
and good foods
seemed to be helping.
Day by day
Kenny acted
a little better.
But he was
still hyperactive.
He slowed down—
but not by much.

Sue felt better
about Kenny.
But Jeff wasn't
so sure.
The reward plan
was a lot of work.
So was watching
what Kenny ate.

Jeff wasn't sure
all the work
was making much difference.
He wanted Kenny
to be like other kids.
So far,
he wasn't.

Thinking It Over

1. Have you ever put yourself on a "reward plan"?

2. What would make a reward plan work for a child?

3. How does food make you feel good or bad?

CHAPTER 5

Jeff and Sue
took Kenny
to visit his grandmother.
The little boy
played in the yard.
Jeff and Sue
sat inside
with Grandma.

"I think
Kenny is much better,"
said Grandma.

"What do you mean?"
Jeff asked.
"Look out that window.
He's still wild.
He still
acts before

he thinks.
He still
can't sit
for more than
two minutes."

"That's better
than before,"
said Grandma.
"He used to sit
for only one minute
at a time.
He's just
a busy boy.
He'll grow
out of it."

"That's what
I used to say,"
said Jeff.

Jeff and Sue
took a walk
around Grandma's yard.

Kenny ran back
to the house.

“May I have
a piece of candy?”
he asked Grandma
as he crashed
through the door.
His parents
couldn’t hear him.

“Be careful, Kenny,”
Grandma warned.
“Slow down or
you’ll have an accident.”
Then she smiled
and handed Kenny
a piece of candy.

Kenny grabbed
the candy
and flew
into the living room.
He ran into

a table.
He knocked off
an old glass bottle.
It made a loud crash
as it fell
to the floor.

Grandma came running.
The blue glass bottle
was in many, many pieces.
"Oh, no!"
she cried.
"That bottle
has been in the family
for so many years.
Now it's gone."
She looked sad.

Jeff and Sue
heard the crash.
They came inside.
They told Kenny
to tell Grandma
he was sorry.

"Maybe he does have
a problem,"
said Grandma.
"I know he didn't mean
to break the bottle.
But he must learn
to slow down."

Thinking It Over

1. Why was it a bad idea
   for Grandma
   to give Kenny candy?

2. How do you feel
   when you have lost something
   you have had for a long time?

3. Why does something bad
   have to happen
   before some people
   believe there is a problem?

CHAPTER 6

Sometimes Kenny
still brought home
good notes
from school.
But he didn't
have any friends.
And he still caused
trouble in class.
And he fell
far behind in his schoolwork.

In the spring
Kenny had a birthday.
He turned
seven years old.
Jeff and Sue
didn't have a party
for him.
They were afraid
he would be

too wild.
Besides, Kenny didn't have
any friends.

Mrs. Pence
called Jeff and Sue.
"Kenny is seven now,"
she said.
"He has not shown
any signs of growing
out of his problem."
Mrs. Pence said
it was time
to think about medicine.
She would talk
to a good doctor.
But first
Jeff and Sue
would have to say
it was OK.

"I just don't like
the whole idea,"
said Jeff.

"Suppose we put him
on drugs now.
When he is older
he might think
all drugs
are OK.
This could lead
to hard drugs."

"That's not likely,"
said Mrs. Pence.
"He'll be taking
this medicine
for a different reason
than people take
hard drugs.
Suppose Kenny
had a heart problem.
Would you still
not want him
to take drugs?
You want him
to learn,
don't you?

You want him
to make friends,
don't you?
Well, for now
this may be
the only way
to help Kenny.
Think about it."

Thinking It Over

1. Why doesn't Kenny
   have any friends?

2. Do you think
   Sue and Jeff
   should have given Kenny
   a birthday party?

3. Why is it time
   to "think about medicine"?

CHAPTER 7

Sue called
Mrs. Pence
on the telephone.
She wanted
to tell Mrs. Pence
how Kenny was doing
at home.
She wanted
to keep
the school
up-to-date.

"He's just a little better,"
said Sue.
"But no children
will play with him.
It's very sad.
But I understand why.
Kenny doesn't know
how to play.

He can't stick
to a game.
I'm worried.
He should have friends
to play with."

"Every child
needs friends,"
said Mrs. Pence.
"Maybe the medicine
will help him
to slow down.
That might help Kenny
make friends.
Have you and Jeff
made up your minds?"

"I don't know
about the medicine yet,"
said Sue.
"But I know
this much.
We will take Kenny
to the doctor."

"How does
Jeff feel
about that?"
asked Mrs. Pence.

"He says
Kenny can go
to the doctor,"
said Sue.
"But he still doesn't like
the idea of medicine."

"Maybe the doctor
will help Jeff decide,"
said Mrs. Pence.

"I hope so,"
said Sue.
"Kenny is my only child.
I want him
to be happy.
I'm willing
to try anything."

"Thank you
for calling,"
said Mrs. Pence.
"I will write
a letter
to the doctor."

Thinking It Over

1. Have you ever felt so bad that you would try anything to make it better?

2. Why is Mrs. Pence writing a letter to the doctor?

3. How would "slowing down" help Kenny to make friends?

CHAPTER 8

Jeff and Sue and Kenny
went to see the doctor.
The doctor explained
some things
about the medicine.
There was
only one way
to know
if the drug would work,
he said.
Kenny would
just have to try it.
The medicine
could help Kenny keep
his mind on things.
Then he could
slow himself down.

"Will the drug
bother Kenny?"
Jeff asked.

"It could," the
doctor answered.

"Will there be any
side effects?"
Sue asked.

"Sometimes there are,"
the doctor answered.
"Kenny may not be
as hungry as he
usually is. Or he
may have trouble
sleeping at night.
But we'll watch him
closely. We can
change the amount
of his medicine
if it bothers him
too much."

"I still don't like
the idea of
my child on drugs,"
said Jeff.

"Do you like
how Kenny acts now?"
asked the doctor.

Kenny was looking
into everything
in the doctor's office.
Jeff told him
to come and sit down.

"No, I don't
like how Kenny acts,"
said Jeff.
"But won't he
grow out of it?"

"Don't kid yourself,"
said the doctor.
"Your son

needs help.
He is falling behind.
And he'll fall behind
even more
without help."

Sue turned to Jeff.
"Let's try the medicine,"
she said.

"OK, OK,"
said Jeff.
"How many pills
must Kenny take?"

Kenny would have
to take
one pill
in the morning.
He would take
a second pill
at lunch.
He would not take
a pill

at night.
He might be able
to go off the pills
in the summer.
If the drug
could work for Kenny,
this plan
would work the best.

Thinking It Over

1. Why should you
   ask a doctor
   before you take certain drugs

2. Can you remember
   ever "kidding yourself"
   about something?
   What made you
   change your mind?

3. Why must there be a plan
   for taking a drug?

CHAPTER 9

Kenny started
to take the pills
the next day.
He took one
at breakfast.
Miss Tiller
made sure
he took
the second pill
at lunch.

Two days later,
Jeff and Sue
could not believe
the change in Kenny.
He seemed happier.
He showed off
his schoolwork.
He felt pleased
with himself.

Jeff and Sue
were very happy.
For the first time
Kenny was acting
like other seven-year-olds.
He didn't run off
when they talked
to him.
He stood still.
He sat
in a chair.
The change
was very clear.

He showed
his parents
his note
from school.
Today he wrote "Yes"
three times,
not just two.

Jeff looked
at Sue.

"I can't believe
it was
this fast and simple,"
he said.
"Why was I so afraid
of the medicine?"

"You were trying
to be a good parent,"
said Sue.
"But I'm glad
you changed your mind.
For the first time
I feel as if
Kenny's going to be OK.
He's not
out of control anymore."

Thinking It Over

1. Why was giving Kenny the dru
   a good idea?

2. Did you ever notice a clear
   change in someone's behavior
   What caused it?

CHAPTER 10

Weeks went by.
Kenny was
learning more.
He was
making friends.
Things were
looking up.

Jeff and Sue and Kenny
went to visit Grandma.
Kenny played
in the yard.
He helped out
in the kitchen.
Then he watched TV
for a whole hour.
He didn't bother
everyone all the time.
He didn't run around
without ever stopping.

The three adults
talked in the kitchen.

"He really is better,"
said Grandma.
"Is it the medicine
that helped him so much?"

"Yes, it is,"
said Jeff.
"The medicine is just
what Kenny needed.
After all,
suppose he had
a heart problem.
He would need
special medicine
for that, right?"

"You have
a point,"
Grandma answered.
"I must say
he's acting a lot better."

"And Mom,"
Jeff went on,
"no candy, please.
Kenny can't handle sweets."

Just then
Kenny came
into the kitchen.
"May I show Grandma
my surprise now?"
he asked.

"Sure,"
said Sue.

Kenny handed Grandma
a present.
"What is this?"
she asked.

Inside the box,
rolled in paper,
was a blue glass bottle.
It looked a lot

like the bottle
Kenny had broken.

"This is beautiful,"
said Grandma.
"Thank you so much."
She gave Kenny
a big kiss.

"We found it
at a yard sale,"
said Sue.

Grandma was
very happy.
"You are
a sweet boy,"
she told Kenny.
Then she put
the bottle
on the table.
It sat
where the old one
had been.

Thinking It Over

1. How can you tell
   things are getting better
   for Kenny and his family?

2. What is a yard sale?

3. Could you love
   the new bottle
   as much as the old one?

CHAPTER 11

Kenny finished
first grade.
He worked very hard
that spring.
He didn't cause trouble
in class anymore.
He was almost
caught up
with the other children.

During the summer
he went
to a special morning class.
He liked school a lot now.
He wanted to be ready
for second grade.
He had to take
one pill a day
in the summer.

Jeff and Sue
were happy that Kenny
was getting along so well.
They made sure
he took his pill.
They didn't want to see
the old Kenny come back.
They liked
the new Kenny better.

One afternoon
Sue and Jeff
were doing some work
around the house.
"Jeff," said Sue.
"I want to tell you
a little secret.
Do you know
why I never wanted
a second child?
It was because
Kenny was so wild.
The way he acted
made me tired

and unhappy all the time.
I didn't know
if I could handle
another child like him."

"I know,"
said Jeff.
"I felt
the same way."

"But now
Kenny is a joy,"
said Sue.
"Now I think
I would like
another baby.
What do you think?"

"I think I like
that idea,"
said Jeff.

Jeff and Sue
held each other.

Together, they looked
out the window
at their son.

Kenny was playing
with his new friend, Bobby.
“Look at me!”
Kenny called.
A happy little boy
was climbing a tree.
He wasn’t climbing
the wall any longer.

Thinking It Over

1. If you had
   a child like Kenny,
   would you want
   a second child?

2. What does it mean
   that Kenny isn't
   "climbing the wall"
   any longer?